THE ATLANTIC WALL	2
HISTORY OF THE CONSTRUCTION OF THE ATLANTIC WALL	4
■ The URSS invasion and the United States' entry into the conflict	5
■ The birth of the wall	7
■ Arrival of Marshal Von Rundstedt	9
■ Fortifications within the 7th Army sector	10
■ 15,000 bunkers and 300,000 men	11
■ The coastal fortification in 1943	12
■ The Atlantic Wall myth	14
■ Rommel and the Atlantic Wall	15
THE TODT ORGANISATION, BUILDER OF THE WALL	18
■ Resistance handout distributed among France's youth	20
■ Collaboration and requisition	20
■ Standardised reinforced concrete blocks	21
MAJOR ATLANTIC WALL SITES IN NORMANDY	23
■ Artillery batteries	23
- La Hague Peninsula	
- The long-range defences of the Cherbourg fortress and Val de Saire	
- Batteries in the Allied landing sector The St Marcouf guns	
- From Cabourg to Dieppe	
■ Infantry structures	29
■ Subterranean galleries	30
■ Detection and radionavigation structures	30
THE WALL, A WARTIME HERITAGE	33

Photo credits: National archives, Washington - Archives Marine nationale, Vincennes – Cabinet des estampes de la BNF, Paris – Bundesarchiv – Koninklijke Bibliothek, den Haag – France Vidéo News, Caen. Philippe Trombetta Collection, Bayeux.

#	Location	#	Location	#	Location
1	Granville (Le Roc)	15	Quinéville (Mont-Coquerel)	28	Bénerville (Mont-Canisy)
2	Vauville (Le Petit-Thot)	16	Saint-Marcouf (Crisbecq)	29	Trouville-sur-Mer
3	Vauville (Les Delles)	17	Azeville	30	Pennedepie (Vasouy)
4	Auderville (Laye)	18	Maisy	31	Bléville
5	Auderville (La Roche)	19	Cricqueville-en-Bessin (Pointe du Hoc)	32	Sainte-Adresse
6	Gréville-Hague (Castel-Vendon)			33	Cap de la Hève
7	Querqueville (Amfreville)	20	Longues-sur-Mer	34	Fontaine-la-Mallet
8	Équeurdreville (Les Couplets)	21	Ver-sur-Mer (Mont Fleury)	35	Ecqueville
9	Cherbourg (Le Roule)	22	Ver-sur-Mer (Marefontaine)	36	Bruneval
10	Tourlaville (Les Caplains)	23	Colleville-Montgomery	37	Fécamp (Senneville et Val Criquet)
11	Fermanville (Hamburg)	24	Ouistreham-Riva-Bella	38	Dieppe
12	Fermanville (La Judée)	25	Ouistreham (Château d'eau)		
13	Gatteville-le-Phare	26	Merville		
14	Crasville	27	Houlgate		

■ Landemer. German fortifications on the coastline in the past, and on the shores today.

THE ATLANTIC WALL

In December 1941, to challenge the imminent Anglo-American landings, Hitler ordered the construction of a line of bunkers along the Western European coastline. In reality, the systematic construction of the coastal rampart was only to begin in the spring of 1942, to be continued without interruption up to June 1944. The Todt Organisation (TO) was chosen to conduct the construction programme devised by Hitler. The TO benefited from the collaboration of a certain number of French building and public works companies. In June 1944, immediately prior to the allied assault on the Normandy shores, in the heart of the Seine Bay, the coastal fortification was far from complete, as can be seen in the Cherbourg sector, Pointe du Hoc or in the former fortress of Le Havre, despite Rommel's numerous inspection rounds.

Today, many significant vestiges remain of the coastal defence system which Goebbels' propaganda was to pompously baptise, the Atlantic Wall. One of the aims of this guide is to introduce readers to the most interesting sites from an architectural, technical or historical point of view, and which can be observed along the Normandy coastline between the Mont Saint-Michel and Dieppe.

Although the German fortified structures bear many similarities (concrete, shape, camouflage...), several types of bunker can nevertheless be identified. The artillery batteries comprising the Wall's backbone were in charge of the long-range defence of the coast. Within the vicinity of the artillery posts, the different structures intended for the infantry, command, transmissions and troop shelter can also be seen. The less familiar subterranean galleries and detection or radionavigation stations are also worthy of interest.

■ Saint-Vaast-la-Hougue. Bunkers in Fort Vauban.

HISTORY OF THE CONSTRUCTION OF THE ATLANTIC WALL

Following France's collapse in June 1940, Hitler was far from imagining the construction of a concrete wall covering the Western European coastline. On the contrary, continuing in his stride, he decided to invade Great Britain, following London's refusal of his proposal for peace. Simultaneously to his preparations to land on the English shores, the *Wehrmacht* staff was devising a plan to invade Spain, with the intention of capturing Gibraltar, hence taking control of the gateway to the Western Mediterranean. In brief, abundant with projects, the German Army multiplied its manoeuvres. Seeking shelter or taking cover along the English Channel coast was not on the agenda.

■ Merville-Franceville. Command bunker with a periscope hole.

■ Quinéville. Tobruk on the banks of the River Sinope.

■ Veys Bay. Double-embrasure bunker

THE URSS INVASION AND THE UNITED STATES' ENTRY INTO THE CONFLICT (JUNE – DECEMBER 1941)

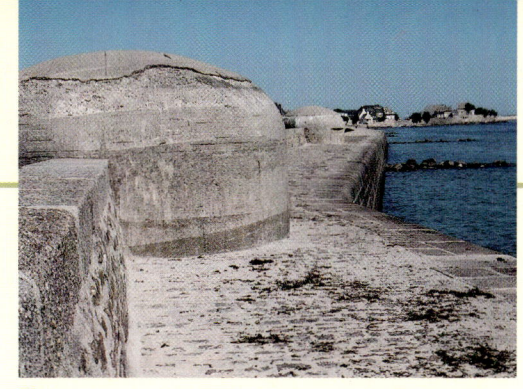

■ Saint-Vaast-la-Hougue. Harbour surveillance fortifications.

Everything was to change in December 1940, with the publication of Hitler's directive ordering the German Army to prepare to invade, as early as the spring of 1941, not Great Britain as everyone expected, but the Soviet Union. From the beginning of 1941, despite continued landing exercises on the English Channel coastline, aimed at obscuring the transfer of German units from the West to the East, the future confrontation with the URSS had became a key concern for all. On the Western Front, abandoning its initial plans to invade, the German Army adopted a defensive attitude and, without for as much developing an overall plan, engaged in the establishment of combat positions along the coastline close to the shore, aimed at countering a hit and run attack or a surprise raid.

■ Cotentin. Watching over the open sea.

■ Sallenelles Bay. Tobruk.

HISTORY OF THE CONSTRUCTION OF THE ATLANTIC WALL

Merville-Franceville. The Third Reich eagle, wings outstretched.

Merville-Franceville. Inscription in German on the concrete base.

Hitler anticipated a short war in Russia, expecting to conclude by late 1941. Endowed with the inexhaustible riches seized from Russia, the Reich could pursue its combat against Great Britain, adjourned late 1940, hence becoming master of Europe. However, they had counted neither on the heroic resistance by the Soviet people, nor on the harsh Russian winter. In December 1941, whilst the *Wehrmacht* had reached a standstill before Moscow, the United States, surprised by the Japanese attack on Pearl Harbour, joined the war (against the Axis powers) alongside Great Britain. Germany found itself trapped on both fronts.

Merville-Franceville. Artillery battery Circular concrete platform.

THE BIRTH OF THE WALL

■ Sortosville-en-Beaumont. *Luftwaffe* structure with the inscription « built under Hitler during the combat against England ».

Whilst the *Wehrmacht* was deep in the heart of the Russian territory and had not yet finished with the Red Army, the American intervention was to abruptly exacerbate the up-and-coming threat on the German Army's rear. On the 14th of December 1941, in order to ward of this, yet distant, danger, Hitler decided to build a line

■ Pointe du Hoc. Bunker after the American aerial and naval bombardments.

of fortifications on the European coast stretching from the North Cape to the Spanish border. Later, the Reich's propaganda services, under Goebbels' command, were to bring to the world's attention this 3,000km long line of fortifications, under the colourful yet deceptive name of *Atlantikwall* or Atlantic Wall.

■ German caricature of Churchill, disappointed by his alliance with Stalin's Russia.

In the spring of 1942, a second directive came to complete the first, ordering to specify the organisation of command on the Western Front and to define the role of each weapon in the coastal protection. However, the key message in this new instruction

HISTORY OF THE CONSTRUCTION OF THE ATLANTIC WALL

■ Artillery battery on the English Channel shoreline.

concerned the defence of the coast. As indicated by Berlin, each coastal sector was to be dealt with according to its strategic value, taking into account the hierarchical order defined in the instruction. The coastal sector which Hitler curiously considered to be the most vulnerable to an amphibious Allied attack was Norway, followed by the coast between the River Escaut and the Seine, then the Atlantic coast stretching from the River Loire to the Gironde and, almost at the end of his list, the Normandy and Brittany shores. Within each coastal sector, the defence was to be concentrated, first and foremost, around major port developments, on the islands just off the coast, then along the long sandy beaches offering propitious conditions for landing troops. According to the directive, all of the coasts were to be defended, from Bayonne to the North Cape, hence inevitably engendering the great dispersal of the German troops. As Frederick the Great said, « He who defends everything defends nothing. »

■ Pointe du Hoc. Observation post.

THE ARRIVAL OF MARSHAL VON RUNDSTEDT

In late March 1942, Hitler named Marshal Von Rundstedt commander in chief of the Western Front, entrusting upon him the mission of successfully building the coastal fortifications. Based on Hitler's instructions, Von Rundstedt defined three types of defensive organisation. He listed 16 portions of the European coastline in the highest ranking category, in other words those involving the sectors most vulnerable to amphibious attack. Within this total, 12 were located on the French coast including Dunkirk, Calais, Le Havre, Cherbourg, Brest, St Nazaire... together with the Channel Islands (Jersey, Guernsey and Alderney). These sectors were to be endowed with powerful defensive systems comprising a concentration of long-range artillery weapons, hence presenting an impenetrable barrier to any assailant. After these 16 defensive sectors, they created *Stützpunkte* or strong points, which were occasionally grouped together. Each strong point established around a secondary port, an estuary or a valuable military facility such as a radar station, was in the form of an independent fortified position under unique command. Each defensive structure was, of course, not equal to an entire defensive sector; however it was sufficiently solid to pose an embarrassing threat to any assailant. And finally, on the first rung of the ladder were the *Widerstandnest* abbreviated to WN (resistance nest). Each WN was a defensive emplacement comprising a few bunkers armed with medium-calibre guns, machine guns or tank turrets placed on concrete bases. For example, in the Utah and Sword beach sector, there were a little over a hundred of such defensive positions located over around 100km of coastline. The famous Longues artillery battery is noted in the German archives under the number WN 48, whereas Pointe du Hoc is listed as WN 75.

■ Portrait of Marshal Von Rundstedt.

■ Longues-sur-Mer. Firing command post.

■ Jersey. Former mill heightened with a concrete tower.

HISTORY OF THE CONSTRUCTION OF THE ATLANTIC WALL

FORTIFICATIONS WITHIN THE 7ᵀᴴ ARMY SECTOR

■ Auderville. Bunker used as a garage.

■ General Dollmann, Commander of the 7ᵗʰ Army (Brittany and Normandy)

In the 7ᵗʰ Army sector, a formation occupying both Brittany and Normandy, the programme involved the construction of 5,000 concrete structures across the 1,570km coastline stretching from the Loire estuary to that of the Dives. Among this total, 2,700 belonged to the German Army, 1,300 to the *Kriegsmarine* (German Navy) and the remaining 1,000 to the *Luftwaffe* (German Air Force). The TO was to build 3,600 bunkers on the Brittany coast and 1,400 in Normandy. The programme comprised four construction stages: the first, and the most important, involved the construction of 2,670 structures, each of the second and third stages involving a thousand. By the end of 1942, 600 of the 2,670 bunkers identified as a priority were complete and as many were under construction, thus representing around 40% of the total programme.

■ Asnelles. Beach defence.

Vauville. Former German quarters.

15,000 BUNKERS AND 300,000 MEN

In August 1942, whilst the war was dragging out in the East, Hitler was increasingly concerned about the Western Front. During a conference aimed at reviewing the Atlantic Wall's progression, the dictator demanded the construction of a total of 15,000 concrete fortifications including a thousand artillery batteries across the 3,000km (as the crow flies) of European coastline. Since each bunker would require a garrison of 20, the operation was to demand a total of some 300,000 men. To this army, needed to be added a strategic reserve of around 200,000 troops comprising essentially Panzer divisions in charge of leading the counter-attack.

In short, to ensure the defence of the Western Front, half a million men would suffice; the equivalent of 50 divisions. Before concluding his conference, Hitler asked Speer, Todt's successor at the head of the agency charged with the construction of the fortified coastal structures, to complete the concreting stage by the 1st of May 1943. In doing so, and in pursuing construction at a breakneck rate, he hoped to stupefy and discourage the Anglo-Americans from attempting any landing operation.

HISTORY OF THE CONSTRUCTION OF THE ATLANTIC WALL

THE COASTAL FORTIFICATION IN 1943

In 1943, thanks to a record production of concrete, the number of defensive positions either complete or under construction progressed from around 5,000 in December 1942 to over 8,000 by late summer 1943; i.e. an average of around 400 bunkers per month! As for the armament positioned along the shoreline, it became increasingly more impressive each day, exceeding 2,500 artillery weapons of a calibre of 75mm or more. Never in the history of the world has man built so much, so quickly. Proud of its success, the TO invited journalists and generals from the Axis' partner nations, including Japan, to take a stroll alongside the Atlantic Wall. Here is an extract from "*L'Illustration*" a French magazine partisan of Nazi Germany, describing the Atlantic Wall, « ...the Wall is even more extraordinary than we had imagined. Its audacious design and the sheer amount of work required for its execution are barely believable. History's sole comparison can be but the Great Wall of China erected on a 3,000km long frontier... Six thousand permanent structures, together with five thousand mobile units are

■ Utah Beach. Projector shelter.

■ Utah Beach. Shelter for troops in the dunes.

■ Vauville. Washbasin under a window.

■ Bruneval. Flak emplacement.

■ Utah Beach. Flanking bunker.

■ Sallenelles. Tobruk.

ready for action. Hundreds of thousands of labourers of various nationalities are occupied in this construction. Two hundred thousand Frenchmen, including a number of volunteers are working on the Atlantic rampart... »

The true figures are naturally inferior to those quoted in the above article aimed at propaganda and brainwashing. According to the German archives, by late 1943, there were a total of 2,700 artillery weapons across the 3,000km coastline stretching from the North Cape to the Pyrenean Mountains.

■ Bunker for an antitank gun. Sallenelles.

■ Ouistreham. Armoured dome.

HISTORY OF THE CONSTRUCTION OF THE ATLANTIC WALL

THE ATLANTIC WALL MYTH

German propaganda was to transform the Wall into a genuine architectural and military legend thanks to cinema. In April 1943, a news report was broadcast illustrating the coastal fortifications in the Pas de Calais region which, as we know, was the most solidly defended sector on the European coast. During the three minute spot, the different stages in the construction of a large calibre battery could be seen: arrival on site of convoys bringing construction materials and manpower, unloading of trucks and railway wagons, laying of metal frameworks on the concrete platform, arrays of cement mixers and concrete pouring, then, instalment of the gun carriage, the gun and the armoured turret.

The scene was concluded with the pouring of the cover slab, site cleaning and the addition of camouflage and a few plants. In a break from the traditional photographic representations, the film, with its animated footage, suddenly appeared to bring the concrete masses to life. Technological modernity, rapid execution, gigantic bunker dimensions, rationalisation of site work... it could all but intrigue the imagination and generate among spectators a sense of confidence, security and invincibility.

■ Saint-Germain-en-Laye. Marshal Von Rundstedt's bunker

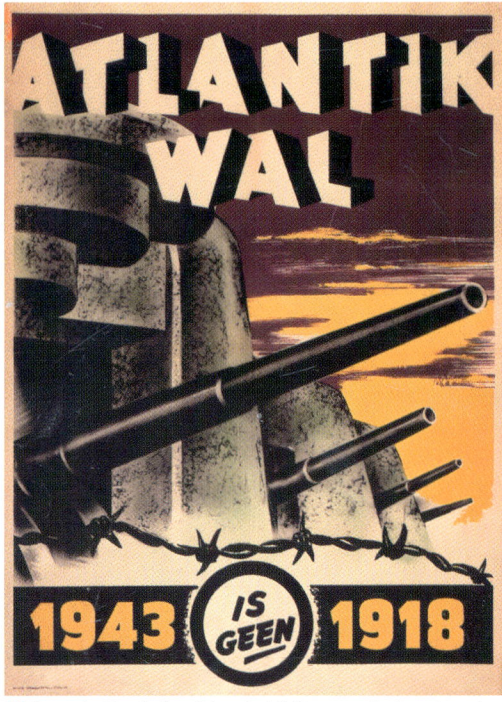

■ Poster in Dutch describing the Wall as an unbroken obstacle.

■ Saint-Germain-en-Laye. Ventilation grids.

ROMMEL AND THE ATLANTIC WALL

At the end of 1943, Hitler, increasingly aware of the threat of an imminent landing, decided no longer to turn his back on Great Britain, but to reinforce the Western Front's defensive potential. To enforce the freshly adopted measures and to revitalise the troops guarding the coast, he named Marshal Rommel Inspector of Coastal Defences, then Commander of Army Group B, a major military formation reuniting two armies north of the Loire (the 7th and the 15th) under one unique command. The Army Group B's mission included repelling the future allied invasion. As for Von Rundstedt, he remained in the same position, but was deprived of part of his command.

■ Omaha Beach. Antitank ditch just behind the beach.

■ Mined beach obstacles.

HISTORY OF THE CONSTRUCTION OF THE ATLANTIC WALL

Although the duration of his command on the Western Front was relatively short, Rommel nevertheless left a significant mark on the coastal defence system. In only six months' command, he was to powerfully reinforce the defence systems on the shorefront, whilst creating a barrier of a certain depth. In order to achieve this, he multiplied the construction of small defensive structures, in particular within concrete niches or tobruks, combat emplacements, trenches and fake battery positions in order to attract enemy bombers. With the aim of bringing the assailants to a halt on the beaches, over and above ditches and antitank walls, Rommel had hundreds of thousands of obstacles placed along the shoreline. Further inland, he planted a proliferation of minefields and, to challenge major airborne operations, had thousands of hectares of land flooded, planting in the prairies tens of thousands of stakes surmounted with mines.

■ Tobruk surmounted by a tank turret.

■ Posts planted in fields to prevent gliders from landing.

All in all, immediately before the Allied landings, the Wall was far from an unbroken obstacle, with the exception of the Pas de Calais and the Somme coasts. In Normandy, apart from the *Festungen* of Le Havre, Cherbourg and the Channel Islands, where an incredible accumulation of concrete could be found, on the rest of the coastline (which as we have already seen was not considered by Hitler as a priority in March 1942), the Wall was but a vast and incomplete building site.

■ Rommel on the Norman front.

■ Obstacle on the beach.

Thanks to these different systems, furiously arranged at the last minute, the Wall was each day to become an increasingly formidable barrier. From January to June 1944, the TO experienced a newfound youth despite the frequent site bombings and the necessity to build further bunkers for launching secret weapons, not accounted for in the initial programme, managing to exceed the figure of 10,000 bunkers disseminated across the Western European coastline.

■ Ouistreham – Remnants of obstacles on the beach.

17

THE TODT ORGANISATION, BUILDER OF THE WALL

After having built the Reich's *autobahn* network in the 1930's, Todt, a public works engineer and one of Hitler's admirers, was entrusted with the construction, opposite the fortified structures comprising the Maginot line, of the 20,000 bunkers of the Siegfried line which at the time the Reich's propaganda had named the Westwall. Following the invasion of France, the military construction agency created by Todt had moved to the Western Front with the mission to erect, in record time, several long-range batteries along the Pas de Calais coastline aimed at protecting the German landing fleet in England, to repair the destroyed airstrips, to build submarine shelters in the Atlantic ports and shelters for speedboats in Cherbourg and Le Havre.

In the spring of 1942, following the death of Todt, the construction staff had been placed under the command of Speer, with a new mission to build a concrete rampart along the Western European coastline, aimed at encumbering and hindering the progression of any assailant. In order to accomplish this gigantic construction programme, the TO had signed contracts with around 200 German public works firms. Most of these major companies had already worked on the *autobahn* or on the Westwall, for which they had built thousands of small bunkers. Incapable of accomplishing alone the defence of the Western European coastline within the deadline set by Hitler, these German companies sub-contracted part of the work to French public works companies. In 1944, an estimated one thousand to one thousand five hundred French public works companies were involved in the TO.

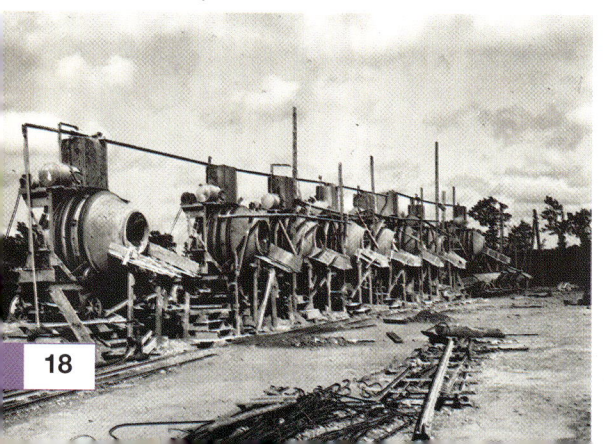

■ Cherbourg. Speedboat shelter filmed by an American cameraman.

■ Sottevast. Array of cement mixers on the giant V2 rocket launching bunker site.

Up to mid 1942, the TO's staff was relatively insignificant. Simultaneously to the initiation of the Atlantic Wall project, the German organisation launched a vast propaganda campaign inviting the French to go and work on the coastal building sites. Focusing on the excellent salaries and the many bonuses the employed volunteers would benefit from, this recruitment campaign succeeded in considerably boosting the agency's manpower. Nevertheless, it remained insufficient and, in 1943, the TO had forced labourers brought to its building sites from the occupied Eastern European territories (Poland, Czechoslovakia, Russia...). Immediately before the D-Day landings, it is estimated that the TO employed some 300,000 labourers on the Western Front, a third of which were French, including many colonials (Moroccans, Algerians, Indochinese...). Considering that the TO had embezzled nine tenths of the French concrete production, that the majority of its manpower was free of charge and that most of the artillery pieces installed in the bunkers were taken from the Maginot line or from French arsenals, we can confirm without doubt that the Atlantic Wall did not represent a major cost for Germany!

■ Cherbourg. TO Offices (late June 1944).

■ Western Cotentin coast. Insignia of the 59th Pioneer Company on the wall of a bunker.

THE TODT ORGANISATION, BUILDER OF THE WALL

RESISTANCE HANDOUT DISTRIBUTED AMONG FRANCE'S YOUTH

In the spring of 1943, whilst Laval requested that the French manpower, in particular those born in 1923, work for the occupant, the *Conseil National de la Résistance* (National Council of the Resistance) did not remain idle before this declaration, launching its own clandestine opinion campaign inviting France's youth to shirk by all means any form of work for the enemy. Below is an excerpt from a handout aimed at renewing confidence and hope among a youth potentially vulnerable to the intense German propaganda conveyed by the Vichy government, and at showing them the way to duty and dignity,

■ Todt Organisation recruitment poster.

«*...the work and the blood of the French belong only to France. They should not be used to prolong the time that separates us from victory, but to reduce it. Each and every young Frenchman must evade the German requisition. Those born in 1923 and whom the invader is endeavouring to mobilise to its advantage are mobilised to serve France. They will work and fight, not for Germany, but against Germany...*»

The Resistance handout went on to encourage France's youth into disobedience, to seeking refuge with relatives living in the countryside or to linking with clandestine movements.

COLLABORATION AND REQUISITION

Among the good thousand French companies working within the TO, certain were in favour of collaborating with the Reich, a great number of others having been requisitioned.

The small core of entrepreneurs willing to contribute towards the German war efforts, those who vehemently called for France's niche in the Atlantic Wall, were to show a scandalous upsurge in their sales figures during their years of collaboration. And since they so spontaneously rushed to serve the enemy, the same entrepreneurs were to stand and justify their acts before the *Commission d'Epuration* (Purge Committee) after the Liberation.

vice) and for Resistant fighters wanted by the Gestapo.

STANDARDISED REINFORCED CONCRETE BLOCKS

The thousands of bunkers erected for the *Wehrmacht* by the TO present significant similarities in terms of the materials used, their architectural form and their interior equipment. The secret of the TO's efficiency was, indeed, its excessive use of standardised structures. Nevertheless, the depth of the walls and of the cover slab depended on each structure's strategic importance: a submarine base or a V-2 rocket launch site benefited from maximum protection against aerial bombing (5 metres

■ Sainte-Croix-Hague. Three directional bunker frameworking.

■ Flanking bunker.

Contrary to those having voluntarily entered into the TO with the intent to facilitate the occupant's initiatives, requisitioned companies were considered, after the war, as having only committed anti-patriotic acts under duress. Requisition enabled business leaders to protect their resources and enabled manpower to avoid being sent to Germany. Once they had joined the TO, many of these companies became sources of information for secret agents working for the Allies or provided shelter both for those having refused the *STO – Service de Travail Obligatoire* (German compulsory work ser-

■ Sallenelles. Observation post.

21

THE TODT ORGANISATION, BUILDER OF THE WALL

Concrete niche or Tobruk for launching grenades.

or often more for U-Boat shelters) The heavy long-range artillery batteries such as St Marcouf, situated inland from Utah beach, had 3.5 metre thick roofs. On the contrary, shelters for troops, ammunition or supplies were covered with a 1.2 metre slab. In all of these fortified structures, concrete was reinforced with a network of round iron wiring laid in three directions. The largest bunkers were built on a thick footing overlapping the concrete cube, hence preventing the structure from toppling in the case of projectiles exploding at the foot of its walls. Furthermore, a layer of earth and stones was placed along the lateral walls to absorb the shock waves caused by any such explosion.

In structures such as command posts, surveillance of the outskirts was ensured via a periscope on the inside and a lookout post on the outside. Shelter entrances were always defended by a firing hole at the far end of the access corridor, the latter being closed behind a double-leaf metal covered door. Certain structures (infirmary, command post, submarine bases...) were equipped with running water and central heating. Shelters used as barracks for troops or as offices were heated using a specially designed stove. The beds in shelters were either wooden or, more commonly, metallic bunk beds on several levels similar to those found in ships.

■ Gold Beach (Asnelles), bunker for an 88mm antitank gun.

■ Utah Beach. Standard defensive bunker on the beach.

■ Caen. German subterranean gallery with metal-covered door.

■ Bunker in the shape of a cube.

MAJOR ATLANTIC WALL SITES IN NORMANDY

With the exception of the Granville batteries, the western coast of the Cotentin peninsula was poorly secured by the occupant, its defensive efforts being concentrated offshore in the Channel Islands. Massively covered in concrete as from 1941, the islands with their heavy artillery batteries, their observation towers, their command posts, their flak emplacements and their subterranean galleries remain, to this very day, a genuine conservatory for fortification enthusiasts, well worthy of a visit.

■ Le Havre. Battery ensuring the long-range defence of the port.

ARTILLERY BATTERIES

Between the Nez de Joburg to the west and the fortress of Dieppe to the east, a great number of more or less preserved vestiges can still be seen of the twenty artillery batteries comprising the Atlantic Wall, each of them entrusted with the long-range defence of a specific maritime sector.

La Hague Peninsula

Although it was inaccessible from the high seas, La Hague was defended by several batteries. The most interesting position is located in the village of Auderville, in the Laye hamlet, one kilometre south of the church. Two large 203mm calibre guns were installed there on railway tracks, capable of firing in all directions at a range of thirty kilometres (20 miles). Although violently bombarded by the US Air Force, the battery is still visible.

■ Fermanville. This is where the German army's heaviest calibre guns on the Normandy coast were to be found.

MAJOR ATLANTIC WALL SITES IN NORMANDY

■ Cherbourg. Bunkers on the slopes of Mount Roule, facing the sea.

Long-range defences in the fortress of Cherbourg and along the Val de Saire coastline

Just like Le Havre, but to a lesser extent, the occupant had transformed the port of Cherbourg into a veritable fortress. Facing the English Channel, the defence systems stretched across several dozen kilometres. There are four particularly interesting structures which are, unfortunately, not open to the public. The Castel Vendon site, edified on land belonging to the French Navy and with its four 150mm calibre guns, is a replica of the Longues battery near Arromanches; the second site in Amfréville, to the west of Cherbourg, is built on military land and comprises 4 large 170mm guns. These two batteries were to successfully repel the Allied fleet on the 25th of June 1944, during the naval bombing of Cherbourg. Within Cherbourg itself, immediately below the Fort du Roule museum, a rather peculiar subterranean battery hollowed within the abrupt escarpment overlooking the city watches over the port to this very day. Finally, in the village of Fermanville, stands the most powerful battery on the entire Normandy coastline. It comprises four old 240mm guns installed within incomplete bunkers. This vast group of bunkers, armed

■ Fort des Couplets. Bunker for a 155mm gun.

■ Gatteville. Bunker for a 155mm gun.

■ Fermanville. Incomplete bunker intended for a 240mm gun.

This inscription confirms that construction of the Merville battery bunkers began in January 1943.

One of the Saint-Marcouf guns in June 1944.

The Saint Marcouf guns

On the morning of the 6th of June at around 5.45am, the large St Marcouf battery (baptised "Crisbecq" by the Americans) guns opened fire on the Fitch and Corry destroyers anchored offshore from the Sainst Marcouf Islands, generating an immediate counter-attack by the two Allied ships which, hence, became the very first to enter into duel with the German coastal guns. Despite this retaliation, the Corry's position rapidly became vulnerable since it was the closest warship to the western Cotentin shores and was also subjected to fire from a second battery, located in Azeville. Furthermore, against the high calibre artillery at Marcouf, comparable to those found on a heavy cruiser, the Corry's 5 inch guns were no match. Each 210mm burst created ever approaching geysers as high as the Corry's mast. Facing the increasing threat, the ship's captain decided to change anchorage and to begin avoidance manoeuvres as quickly as possible. Despite these disorderly movements, the Corry was hit at 6.33 am by two or three 210mm shells which exploded inside the vessel, flooding the engine rooms, putting out the lights and blocking the rudder. The Corry finally broke in two and sunk. After having jumped overboard, the ship's crew who, despite the strong currents, attempted to swim away from the wreck under incessant enemy fire, was eventually rescued 2 hours later. A little over 50 seamen (killed or wounded) were missing from the ship's 250-man strong crew. Curiously, official American history recounts that the Corry was not, in fact, hit by enemy guns but that it had run into a mine. Very probably a matter of self-esteem! All of the above taken into account, the efforts provided by the German coastal guns on the morning of the 6th of June were nevertheless mediocre.

with long-range guns which also participated in the naval duel on the 25th of June 1944, is not open to the public. To the west of Gatteville, the Néville headland is a fine example of one of the Wall's strong points. Several bunkers can be seen surrounded by many other defensive structures. Within the vicinity of the Gatteville lighthouse, the occupant had built a battery with a telemetry post nearby. This easily accessible site is of particular interest.

Batteries within the Allied landing sector

In the Allied assault sector, between Utah and Sword (80km), half a dozen German coastal artillery positions can still be seen. The heavy artillery battery in St Marcouf (four 210mm Skoda guns), located alongside the D69 minor road next to the hamlet of Crisbecq, was the most powerful artillery position within the Seine Bay (between Cape Barfleur and the Antifer headland). On the morning of the 6th of June 1994, just before 6am, these Czechoslovakian guns were to fire on the US Corry destroyer positioned off Utah beach. This site, well worth a visit, offers explanatory display panels. On the same occasion, the nearby and well-preserved Azeville battery, is also worth a detour.

25

MAJOR ATLANTIC WALL SITES IN NORMANDY

With the exception, of course, of the American cemetery in Colleville-sur-Mer, the coast's most moving and captivating site is without a doubt Pointe du Hoc (six 155mm guns) capable of attacking out to the high seas. Similarly to the neighbouring military cemetery, Pointe du Hoc, where a US Army commando earned its everlasting renown, is the property of the United States government. It is one of the D-Day landing route's finest examples of site conservation. A few kilometres from there, to the west of Arromanches, the Longues-sur-Mer battery, with its German guns of a range of 20km (12 miles) and its firing command post located in the foreground, immediately overlooking the shore like a warship, is not be missed (guided tours available). In Ouistreham, the large firing command post from the former battery, now covered, has been transformed into an interesting Atlantic Wall museum. On the opposite bank of the River Orne, in the village of Merville, just behind Franceville, stands a battery which, despite the size of its bunkers, only contained 4 medium-range guns at the time of the Allied landings. This position was attacked by the British 6th Airborne Division's paratroops on the night of the 5th to the 6th of June. The visit can be completed with a trip to the nearby museum which boasts both a Dakota plane, specialised in dropping paratroopers, and a perfect replica of a Horsa glider cockpit.

■ Merville. Merville Battery with its four bunkers.

■ Longues. Bunker for 150mm German gun.

■ Merville. Bunker protected on each side by a mound of earth.

Benerville. Cubic bunkers intended for 15.5cm guns and located at the summit of the Mont Canisy mound.

Concrete platform at the Pointe du Hoc Battery.

From Cabourg to Dieppe

Although located outside the traditional D-Day route, the Mont Canisy battery, in the town of Bénerville, near to Deauville, is an exceptional site. Situated on a mound, at an altitude of 110 metres, it is a perfect example of a *Stützpunkt*. Over and above the battery itself, with six 155mm guns, as in both Ouistreham and Pointe du Hoc, the artillery position also comprises a hundred or so different defensive structures scattered over several hectares. The highpoint of the guided tour is the discovery of a subterranean gallery including thirty rooms (barracks and ammunition holds). Acquired by the *Conservatoire du Littoral* (French coastal conservation agency), the former artillery position has benefited from high quality preservation thanks to the skill of the very competent *Amis du Canisy* association. Closer to the Seine estuary, located between Pennedepie and Honfleur, the Vasouy battery with its two floor firing command post is identical to the Longues battery.

Ouistreham. Former firing command post, transformed into a museum.

27

MAJOR ATLANTIC WALL SITES IN NORMANDY

■ Bléville la Corvée. 380mm gun.

Immediately prior to the D-Day landings, the Le Havre *Festung* was one of the Atlantic Wall's strongest and most strategic links. Within the fortress, the occupant had built some 400 bunkers, a great number of which have today disappeared (bombardments, demolition, covering, urbanisation...) or are encompassed within the vast port area. For example, the formidable structures designed to house 380mm gun turrets in the village of Bléville-la-Corvée have been completely covered. The bunkers of the naval battery (four 170mm guns) located in Bléville are among the most impressive vestiges still visible today. Further batteries can be seen in Ecqueville, in the Ste Adresse Fort and in the village of Fontaine-la-Mallet (Mont Trottin and Mont Fèvretôt). Below the Ste Adresse Fort, in Rue Chef de Caux, stands the former command post of the German general in command of artillery for the entire Le Havre sector. It is a vast and striking three-level fortification with an outstanding view of the open sea. In the town of Fécamp, the local heritage coordination department organises guided tours of German fortifications including the former Senneville battery and the Val Criquet subterranean gallery. In Dieppe, where the occupant had built around 200 bunkers, the most interesting structures are the detection facilities, the subterranean galleries and the fake bunkers painted on the cliff side.

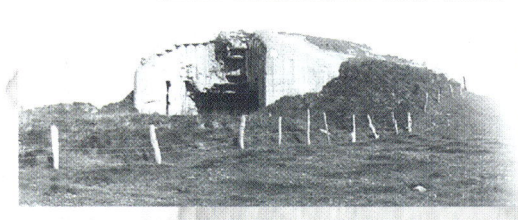

■ Bléville – Large bunker for a modern, 170mm gun.

Dieppe. Fake firing hole on the cliff.

INFANTRY WORKS

Over and above the artillery batteries designed for long-range defence, the *Wehrmacht* had also built hundreds of fortifications aimed at the close-range defence of the shoreline, in other words, at repelling any assailant having succeeded in setting foot on the beaches. These structures were armed with antitank guns, heavy machine guns, grenade launchers or outdated French tank turrets. Other bunkers were used as barracks for the troops, as ammunition holds and as garages or shelters for guns and standard or armoured vehicles. There are fine examples of infantry-armed strong points at the Néville headland (within the vicinity of the Gatteville lighthouse), inland from Utah beach (St. Martin-de-Varreville), on Omaha beach (WN 62 near the American cemetery), in Colleville-Montgomery (strong point baptised Hillman by the British) today developed by a highly active association which organises site visits, together with Mont Canisy, near Deauville.

Antitank wall on the coastline.

Tollevast. Turret on the top of a bunker.

29

MAJOR ATLANTIC WALL SITES IN NORMANDY

SUBTERRANEAN GALLERIES

■ Guernsey. Underground hospital dug out by the TO's forced labourers.

The TO dug out numerous subterranean galleries along the Normandy coastline, the most impressive of which can be found in the Channel Islands. The La Vassalerie gallery, in Guernsey, which was used as a military hospital for German soldiers injured on the Normandy front in June 1944, is approximately 2km in length. In Cherbourg, an important subterranean gallery (closed to the public) was the fortress's commander, General Von Schlieben's command post. He surrendered to the Americans late June 1944. The commander of the German 716th Infantry Division, General W. Richter's former command post is located under the Caen Memorial museum, hollowed from a former quarry face. Subterranean galleries can also be found in the *Vaches Noires* (Black Cow) cliffs in Auberville, under the Mont Canisy, in Le Havre (under the Mont Joly) and in Dieppe (under the castle and at Le Pollet).

DETECTION AND RADIONAVIAGATION STRUCTURES

Because of their proximity to the English coast, the Channel shores in France were equipped with a number of radar and radionavigation stations.

Between La Hague and Dieppe, a dozen electromagnetic detection stations can be found,

■ Cherbourg. Entrance to General Von Schlieben's underground command post.

■ Cherbourg. Inside General Von Schlieben's command post. In the small picture, the Auberville subterranean passage.

30

■ Dieppe. Mammut radar antenna.

■ Carneville. Vestiges of the *Luftwaffe's* large radar station.

equipped with different types of antenna. The Mammut, name given to the long-range *Kriegsmarine* radar, was easily recognisable thanks to its huge rectangular antenna, whereas the Freya, many examples of which can be found along the coast, was a medium-range device. Wassermann (equipped with a narrow and very high antenna) and Würzburg-Riese (recognisable thanks to its parabolic antenna) radars were used by the *Luftwaffe*.

The most important radar camps are located in La Hague, where to this very day a concrete vat can be seen within the Auderville battery (La Roche hamlet), which formerly housed a Freya radar; similarly, in the nearby village of Digulleville (in the locality of Gouesneraie) a shelter surmounted by three concrete cubes which were once a base for a Mammut radar. A heathy slope in the village of Carneville, on the north coast of the Cotentin peninsula, east of Cherbourg, is home to the vestiges of a vast *Luftwaffe* radar station, once equipped with several devices, each of which was set to a different wavelength in order to counter the Allied radar jamming. A smaller detection station was located at Pointe de la Percée, just to the east of Omaha beach, and another on the cliff overlooking Arromanches. The major *Luftwaffe* radar fortress located in the town of Douvres-la-Délivrande (to the northwest of Caen), in the very heart of the D-Day landing sector, was to suffer

MAJOR ATLANTIC WALL SITES IN NORMANDY

■ St. Pierre-Eglise. Former radionavigation station.

severe bombardments and radar jamming immediately prior to the Allied assault. In Le Havre, the *Kriegsmarine* had set up a powerful station at Cap de la Hève, whereas, for the surveillance of the airspace, the air force used the radar camps in Bruneval and the substantial station in Dieppe (remnants of which can be seen on the golf course in the form of concrete cubes, formerly housing a Mammut radar, at the summit of Mont Robin).

The German radionavigation stations, which were also equipped with huge antennas, were not used for detection but to provide land-based guidance for swastika bombers over the English towns. Several systems were used by the occupant, all of them benefiting from one or several antennas set up on circular concrete bases located next to the bunkers which provided shelter for their generators. This was the case in Sortoville, on the west Cotentin coast, and in Beaumont-Hague, in St. Pierre-Eglise (alongside the 801 road, where the 6 antennas were partly supported by pylons and partly by the bunker cover slab), on the La Pernelle heights and, finally much further inland, on the Mont Pinçon in Calvados, within the immediate vicinity of the *France Télévisions* transmitters.

■ La Pernelle. Radionavigation station transmission antenna.

■ Concrete cubes intended to house a large radar antenna. Fécamp.

32